I Belong Deeply to Myself

Dallas Taylor

ISBN: 9798853429482

Cover art by Nikki Gomez @nikki_ink_ & Kate McCall
Photos by Kate McCall @katemcallll
Edited by Kate McCall, Morgan Watkins, & Sydney Fuller

DEDICATION

For the girls, and for Gunner, but especially for
my sister, Kate, who looks a lot like Love.

"I belong deeply to myself."

-WARSAN SHIRE

CONTENTS

Proximity to the Undoing of Love

I Belong Deeply to Myself

I grew up in a house on fire, where two golden rings
had become Trojan horses, used to attack the enemy at
their weakest points from the inside out. Our home
became another house for sale and the music that once
played in our kitchen was drowned out by a symphony
of shattered glass and spilt liquor. I watched Anger and
Guilt devour my father, while Shame and Fear split my
mother in half. Determined not to meet their same fate,
I buried my own feelings as deeply as I could.
Eventually, though, they unearthed themselves. They
aired their grievances all at once, "You've lost me!"
exclaimed Joy. "You never hear me," quipped Sadness.
Guilt sat in the corner with a murderous smile and
chuckled, "I've been waiting for this." Doubt crept over
my shoulder and whispered, "You'd better give up
now…" Fear nodded in agreement while Anger shouted
unintelligibly. Grief and Love sat quietly, speaking
amongst themselves, throwing me an occasional glance.
I tried to drown them out the way I had so many times
before, but a pain in my side let me know I was
bleeding. I could no longer outrun them. All I could do
was *listen*.

The undoing of love is a complex thing. So many feelings are wrapped up in love that when it cracks, all of the emotions pour out into the room and contradict each other. Lust and Anger dance together with knives tucked up their sleeves, ready to strike at a moment's notice. Sadness and fear whisper to each other about the future while Shame self-deprecates. Guilt and Disgust try to place blame, but aren't sure whose it is to carry. Jealousy waits in the dark, prepared to knock the wind out of us when we think we've found our footing. The longer we wait to address them the louder they get, until we're stuck in a cacophony of our own making.

In my childhood home, Fear never tucked itself away in closets or under beds. It didn't lurk in the dark waiting for the opportune moment, nor did it cower to my night-light. Fear and I were so familiar, I mistook it for a friend. It ran behind me in P.E. races, yelling, "Faster! Faster!" It carved its name next to mine on the honor roll and smiled as we won class clown but whispered, "Do you think they were laughing with you or *at* you?" I built shadow boxes and trophy shelves, hoping Fear would notice our accolades and finally quiet down, but it turned up its nose and scoffed, "Not enough!" Exhausted, I asked, "What *is* enough, Fear?" It had no answer for me, and I realized it never would, for Love would be the one to teach me that.

Anger is my father in the middle seat of an airplane. It is cumbersome and uncomfortable. I avoid it with faked niceties like a good stewardess, confident that if I circumvent it until after the beverage service, its fury will subside. This hardly ever works, though. Anger festers in its seat, its bitterness growing with every passing moment. When I settle in to read a good book, it bubbles up inside me, hitting my invisible call button incessantly until I am forced to hear its cries. I approach it slowly, cautiously even, but when I reach it, I realize all it really wants is to be listened to.

Sadness is an old, solemn woman who means no harm, but sometimes sits on my chest and makes it hard to breathe. She is the great matriarch of my Italian-Greek-Irish family, who holds all the wisdom of where we come from in her handwritten recipe books; one part shame to two parts pride, heated over three generations until boiling. Her silent sacrifice went unnoticed by so many, while I watched the others roll their eyes, writing her off as over-dramatic. But I listen to her stories, for I know my sadness has much to teach me, even if she was not mine to begin with.

My shame became a fixture in every home I made for myself. I clung to it like a family heirloom (because after all, it was), and introduced it to my houseguests who marveled at its size. It sat on my shelves like the tchotchke of an eccentric great aunt—a statement piece and an eyesore all in one. When I set my eyes east, though, I realized I couldn't possibly take it with me. It was too large and too cumbersome to strap to the top of my car, and New York apartments are notoriously small. I took my shame and sent it down the river as an offering to the God I'd been taught to fear. As I watched it float away toward Babylon, I realized both of us were finally homeward bound.

Rest has a shadow whose name is Guilt. It is the insufferable know-it-all who *loathes* comfortable silence. When Rest and I are trying to enjoy a quiet moment alone, Guilt interjects with, "Did you know it takes 10,000 hours to master a skill? How many would you say you've spent writing? I'd bet it's fewer." Rest and I roll our eyes, but the truth is, we're afraid Guilt is right. Should we be using this time *better*? Should we be doing *more?* What if this moment is precious and we're wasting it? As Rest and I try to shut our eyes at night, Guilt sits in the corner, sharpening its nails, "Remember when you did a *horrible*, ignorant, awful thing?" I won't let Guilt make me its next meal. I roll over, turning my back to Guilt and its insatiable appetite.

"We'll always do worse before we know better."

Guilt goes to bed hungry.

Grief is a friend disguised as a foe. The entire time she's in front of you, you curse her, willing yourself to be rid of Grief and all of her heaviness. You fight with her constantly, shouting, "You're too much!" But Grief persists. Her voice rises above your own with a cynical, "I'm not going anywhere." We swear she is plotting our downfall, forcing us to meet parts of ourselves we were too ashamed to claim. One day without warning, she quiets down, slips out the back without another word, and stops taunting us with our fear of the dark. We don't notice she's gone until those parts of ourselves we had tucked away seem less looming, and suddenly we realize that Grief was, in fact, a friend. She was always rooting for us, and she forced us to fall in love with our shadows.

I Belong Deeply to Myself

Self Doubt is the biggest monster in my closet. It sits on my shoulders when I send an invoice and snickers at me in a low, gray voice, "Are you sure you're worth that much?" It whispers obscenities in my ear when I consider asking for help, "Why would *they* help *you?*" A maniacal grin spreads wide across its face as it knows it has me *exactly* where it wants me. I flinch at the cold touch of its iron fist around my throat when someone asks me what I do. Self Doubt wants me to choke out, "I write," instead of confidently stating, "I am a writer." It is a gargoyle at the gates of my mind who intends to scare away any opportunity, connection, or outsider, and I'm getting really tired of its slow and dreadful lurch. I can tell I'm close to finding the night light to scare it away for good, it's just going to take a little more searching in the dark.

My pride was a gargantuan bully, a popular girl in every way, completed by her nasty sidekick, my ego. They gloated through the hallways together, sneering at Humility and the way she asked for help. "Not for us!" they laughed boisterously. I liked the way I looked at their table during lunch; cool and unaffected, our polished manicures a testament to the fact that, we had never held onto anything too tightly. Humility had chipped nails and undone hair. She looked weak and even a little pathetic. I felt sorry for her, until one day I heard her laughing. I turned to find her seated next to Love, and together they were messy, imperfect and *real*. The light I had once seen Humility in had changed–she wasn't weak, she was honest. She wasn't pathetic, she was kind. I decided at that moment to swallow my bullies whole. They went down something wicked and still kick within me from time to time, but I'm here, at the table with Love and Humility. They've taught me the coolest girls are the ones who aren't afraid to look a little silly in the pursuit of a life well-lived.

I Belong Deeply to Myself

Love found me at the sushi restaurant with no life behind my smile. Cascading curls framed her deep brown eyes, and as I searched them for pity, I found compassion in its place. Her smile was laced with courage, and it gave me the confidence to try again. She held my hand through thunderstorms, and made me brave as we picked up pieces of my broken heart from the deserts of Arizona and New Mexico. Love's infectious laugh became the song of the summer, and we sang it across the Great Plains of Texas and over the Smoky Mountains of Tennessee. We shouted it from rooftops in the French Quarter and boot-stomped to it on Music Row. As Love giggled beside me, I caught a glimpse of someone I'd forgotten in the rear view mirror. Love had invited Joy, and I was finally ready to welcome her.

When I finally decided I deserved to know Joy, I was surprised to find so much of myself in her. Her cheeks were much rosier than mine–flushed from a night spent dancing to the songs I sang in middle school. My hands, meticulously manicured, looked nothing like hers–with hot pink paint splattered across them. Her laugh was louder. She looked at me, confused, as if she saw herself in me, too, and asked, "what *happened* to you?" I stared back at her, puzzled, and she continued, "Why are you so *gray*?" I looked down at my boring slacks and take-me-seriously loafers. I shrugged. It seemed as if all I had done for the past five years was shrug. She grabbed her hot pink paint and dumped it over my head. Fuchsia trickled across my perfectly pressed shirt. She reminded me that I used to do things just because I liked them. Joy took me over mountains and across seas. She taught me how to paint without worrying over what the picture would look like. I learned how to eat and live and *feel* again. While I wasn't looking, my gray, lonesome, little life turned big and technicolor.

I Belong Deeply to Myself

Every feeling has something to teach us—if we let them. When we try to bypass Anger and its fiery wrath for fear of burning up in its flames, we deprive ourselves of the rebirth to be found in its ashes. When we attempt to ignore Grief like a storm outside, we forgo the opportunity to be drenched in the reminders of how deeply we have loved. Some feelings are heavier than others, and it can be tempting to disinvite Shame, Fear, Jealousy, Sadness, Loneliness, Anxiety and Apathy from the party in favor of more chipper guests like Happiness, Love, Pride, Hope, Pleasure, Gratitude and Joy. When you welcome every emotion to the table, though, you give yourself the chance to find the *whole* truth. You give yourself the chance to find *compassion.*

Fine! I Care! A Lot!

Admitting you care about something is *terrifying*, because admitting what you want is the first step in actually *getting* what you want. It requires vulnerability, and therefore, risk. You risk being left alone in the wanting. You risk losing the hope that lives within the dream of what you want. Turning your dream into a reality entails potential embarrassment, loss, and sometimes, pain. Here's a secret, though: there's no shame in caring. When you admit to the things you care about, you put yourself in a position to get what you want. It's a risk, but admitting you care is a bet you make on yourself. Once you decide you deserve the things you want, you will get them one way or another, because you're betting on the house, and the house *always* wins.

I grew tired of acting like I cared less. I had learned this philosophy, maybe from my peers or maybe from the internet, that somehow the person who cared the least was the winner. But really, if caring less is winning, what's the prize? Apathy? Emptiness? Being unbothered? If someone breaks me in half, they will hear me cry. If they light me up inside, they will feel the warmth in my words. I want to spend my life *creating* my life, and I want to decorate it with people who care just as much as I do. My life is for me. It is my chance to enjoy beautiful moments, learn as much as I can, and revel in the phenomenon of being alive. If the contest is caring less, I forfeit, and those who care less about me forfeit their spot in my wonderful little life.

I used to be *obsessed* with the idea of moving with grace. I would approach every situation with the intention of making as few waves as possible, hoping to leave a sweet, delicate imprint in my wake. I mostly tried to do this in situations where I had been hurt. I wanted the opportunity to see the people who had hurt me regret their actions. I wanted them to look back on the hurt they caused me and be impressed by my lack of reaction. As time went on, though, I realized I wasn't so much moving with grace as I was bottling everything up. And the people who had hurt me? Well, I learned a hard truth about people who are willing to discard you or cross you for their own benefit; they don't care. Sometimes, people *just don't care.* After I had made peace with this revelation, I let go of my need to be perfectly posed and rehearsed, unheard and unbothered. I decided it was more important to me to be honest than to be graceful. Personally, I have found more true grace in honesty than I did in silence and demure.

I still remember my first boyfriend's birthday and the songs we'd sing together on drives home from the beach. I remember all of my boyfriend's birthdays for that matter. I remember the street my second boyfriend lived on because I used to send him love letters. I remember the way he loved cheesecake and hope he gets one every year on his birthday because it's his favorite. I remember the way the last boy I dated hated sneezing and loved his mother and I still hope she gets her promotion and that his grandpa gets to retire. I think I'm the kind of person who will always remember and who will always care. Maybe it's my curse or maybe, it's my gift.

I think the most courageous thing anyone can be is a try-hard. To look at the world we live in—a world that celebrates effortlessness over candor, detachment over care, and power over earnestness—and choose to be frank about the things that break us open is brave. That bravery requires a weapon that is not an axe to be thrown or a sword to be wielded. It's an invisible cloak we must shed to be truly seen, a special kind of strength we must learn over and over again in different forms. It requires *vulnerability.*

I tried to find self care in the neatly wrapped packages being sold to me, full of face masks and green juices. I looked for it in steadfast discipline, hoping to work away the gray feeling that lived in the pit of my stomach. When that didn't work, I thought maybe days spent in bed or throwing my diet out the window would help. It didn't. *Real* self care showed up when I started nurturing the little girl inside of me. Nurturing her requires balance. I make her brush her teeth, even when she'd rather run out the door in a haste. Sometimes, I feed her green juice, because it's good for her. Other times, I feed her chocolate cake because it's *also* good for her. I play with her, dance with her, and believe in her. I'm patient with her, because she's still learning. Most nights I make sure she gets enough sleep, and occasionally I stay up late with her to jump on the bed. I let her dream big because I know she is capable. I tell her we are strong, we are loved, we are worthy of good things, and we are beautiful. I smile because I know she believes it now, too.

Tell people you love them. Tell them that you're proud of them. Tell them you believe in them. *Especially* the people you think don't need to hear it. Say it again when they brush you off, or when they turn away from you in a way that lets you know it's been far too long since they've heard it. Say it until they look you in the eyes and know you *mean* it. The people who set you on fire deserve to know how brightly they burn.

I don't want a love I achieve through smoke and mirrors. I don't want to con my way into a forever using carefully calculated dance steps or a mysterious facade. I want to show up as me, *all of me*, and be loved out in the open. No tricks, no sleight of hand, just two people brave enough to be all of themselves with each other.

The Second Heartbreak

The second heartbreak called me his Mona Lisa, a two-dimensional beauty he could hang from the wall and marvel at. He paraded guests around my glass case to make himself feel important. For a time, it made me feel important, too. But he hated the sound of my cries, unless they were in a key he found inspiring. He angered at my human movements, and the inevitable, troublesome enlightenment that came with my aging, sneering, "*just stand still.*" Being a muse had sounded fun, romantic even. Then, I learned some artists won't paint you as you are, they'll paint you as they wish you to be.

I Belong Deeply to Myself

You once told me I was an earthquake of a human being whose presence filled up every room. I think for a moment, my power didn't scare you because you thought you could confine it in your hands and make it *yours*. But this force within me has always been mine, and mine alone. I'm sorry I couldn't be the magic mirror to reflect you twice your size. It's not in my nature, you said it yourself.

I'm meant to shake people to their core.

The Third Heartbreak

Before I called him my third heartbreak I called him a friend of a friend. He began as a whisper on the lips of someone I trusted, and with a simple, "I think you two would get along," the story was set in motion. Soon, I'd call him every night, to hear what he thought about what was on the news or to tell him how I liked the songs he sent me. Before I called him my third heartbreak, I called him first thing in the morning. I called him baby. I called him from the bathroom to ask for a towel. Even still, I never called him *mine*—and so, the third heartbreak was born.

When I told him I was excited to show him more parts of myself, he responded with, "I've already seen everything there is to see." I looked at him, confused because we'd only been dating a few months. He continued, "I've already seen you naked." That's when I realized I had been looking at his soul while he had stopped at my body.

I Belong Deeply to Myself

Pretty, lifeless, drunk proclamations are not love.

"Maybe," is not love.

Love is respect, and respect doesn't leave you guessing.

Respect doesn't make you wait up at night, terrified they've found someone they like better at a party.

Respect doesn't take back the drunk words they told you with their hands on your thighs.

Respect shows up.

Respect listens.

When he finally decided to show me some decency and leave me, I realized what was possibly the most painful part of it all;

The respect I had been starved of had mostly been my own.

My hair fell around us like the curtain of my favorite show, leaving me screaming "Encore! Encore!" and electrifying me in the way only theater can. I sat in the dark, long after everyone had gone home, and wondered aloud if I had imagined it all. For you, it was the performance of a lifetime. For me, it was real.

I Belong Deeply to Myself

I romanticized the boy until the man in my head was unrecognizable. He was strong and honest, charismatic and respectable. I admired him so ardently, but every time I tried to hold him close, the boy wriggled out from under me and reminded me that what I was seeing wasn't there. I think the boy caught glimpses of his own reflection in my eyes, and thought for just a moment he could become the man who lived in my head. Ultimately, the character I'd written for him put his real character to shame. He ran off with his tail between his legs, and I had to admit the real reason I had spent so much time writing his story was because I was too scared to write my own.

Somewhere in Scottsdale, there is a version of me who lives in the closet of that old apartment on 78th street. She is neatly placed on the second shelf to the right where I used to keep my things. She has freshly shaved legs and smells like strawberry shampoo. She thinks there will be peaches with dinner, and she can't wait for you to get home. No one has the heart to tell her you don't live there anymore. I couldn't take her with me. She wouldn't have left if I tried.

I kissed him like I was desperate to keep him. I held on by my teeth to the lips I was convinced would change it all. I tried to bury my finger tips in his back to keep my grip on the man I could feel slipping away and I let him live in my bones, hoping he would find my flesh comfortable enough to stay. I set myself on fire trying to keep him warm, then had the nerve to act surprised when I found myself burned. I kissed him like I was desperate to keep him, *because I was*.

It wasn't until months later I realized fate hadn't brought us together, we had just collided momentarily on our separate ways toward what each of us was meant for. I was running away from home, desperate for an escape, and he was out on his own, looking for stability to cling to. I had to find my own exit route just like he had to find his own solid ground. We had tried to make life rafts out of each other, and he had been the first one to learn how to swim.

I'm sorry — it's just that the way you said, "I love you," sounded like the door my father used to slam and the smell of your skin took me home, where nothing was good but everything was familiar. Your golden eyes hung over me like the light of the childhood bedroom I knew was somehow temporary and forever all at once. I really didn't mean to hurt you, I just thought we could go together, out of that old house and out to sea. I thought if I could fix you the way I hadn't fixed them, it would somehow take this pain I inherited and turn it into something better, brighter even. But you aren't a home and I'm not a child, and to put it plainly, I'm proud. I'm proud because even though we were just ships passing in the night, each of us made it out to sea. Even if it couldn't be together.

I wish you gentle waters.

Do you remember the sweet boy in glasses and mismatched socks? You know, the one who came out when I told him it was safe to stop hiding? Or, who sat with me at the red rocks and told me he was scared? The one who looked at me with gentle eyes and a whipped cream sort of softness I've been in search of since? Did his tenderness scare you? Was it easier to pretend you'd never known either of us? How did it feel to hear him cry while you laughed it off with your buddies? I hope you didn't tell him he was crazy. I hope he didn't cut himself on the jagged glass from the mirror you shattered in an effort to send him away. I hope you didn't bury him the way you buried me. I hope you hold him close. I wish I could. He was *magic*.

I Belong Deeply to Myself

I once hoped for the chance to drink your regret like wine. I pictured us at our friend's wedding, me in my best dress and you in your shame. I thought you'd apologize and I'd get to bask in the glory of your remorse. The smooth flavor I had imagined for your guilt was replaced by a burn in the back of my throat when I saw the woman who had come after me—beautiful, talented, incredible—like so many of us are. I realized then that someone who never considered me when we were together wasn't going to do it in my absence. I sent my need for revenge an eviction notice and watched as people flooded into the space you once occupied—friends who remember my birthday and listen when I'm talking. A lover who opens my doors, even when it's to leave him.

People who treat me like I treated you.

Dallas Taylor

Though I'll never let the world harden me, or allow myself to be closed off from love, light, or pain, there is a grit in my softness. My hands still know how to hold, but they rest in fists. I am no longer a saccharine confection dressed up in ribbons for consumption. My fire burns brightly but it is not intended to warm—it's a warning; do not pretend to love me if you have no intention of meaning it. I will never love someone the way I loved you—hopelessly, powerlessly, foolishly— because I care far too much about the girl within me who once gave away her light as decorations for an altar.

Sometimes love comes into our lives for just a moment to wake us up but isn't meant to stay. Be grateful your eyes opened, even if it stings.

I think if I were born a man I'd be a preacher in a mega church. I speak with great conviction and have a flair for the dramatic. I'm persuasive, stubborn, and I *hate* to be wrong. I almost always *truly* believe my heart is in the right place, even when I'm being self-indulgent, greedy, or callous. So believe me when I say it pains me to admit…

…you were right.

I was wearing my headset microphone and flying around the stage creating a real spectacle of myself, begging you to worship at the altar of false Gods; the ones I had made out of two scared kids who'd stumbled into the same purgatory at the same time. I called you a non-believer and wrote you a Sinner's Prayer for leaving limbo before I could. I won't take all the blame though, after all, it was you who cut the line while I was mid-backflip trying to rally the congregation—turns out, it *does* hurt to fall from Heaven. The choir and the organ came together to mourn with me, and just as I began to fashion myself into the martyred, fallen archangel, I was struck by the painful, and yet righteous revelation that I had mercilessly used you, too.

Peace be with you.

To All the Boys I Blamed Before

The weight of my perceived desirability was immense,
carrying with it years of stern reminders;
Don't wear too much makeup, boys don't like that.
Don't cut your hair short, boys don't like that.
Don't be too easy, but don't be too hard to get.
Don't have too much weight on you, but don't be too
skinny.
Don't care too much, but don't care too little.
Be sexy, but not slutty.
Be friendly, but not too approachable.
Be funny, but not funnier than them.

Boys. Don't. Like. That.

I meticulously studied the blueprint I was presented
with in magazines whose glossy covers shouted at me
from grocery checkout lines,

"SEDUCE HIM INTO STAYING!" "BLOWJOBS TO
BLOW HIS MIND!" "YOU'RE FAT? HE'S GONE!"

I learned my own sex appeal was the currency with
which I was to buy respect. I had to have enough to be
considered, but not so much that I wouldn't be taken
seriously. I spent decades of my life parading around
like show cattle, praying to be bid on, blissfully
unaware the blue ribbon came with a butcher. First I
trimmed away the fat, then the sense of humor, the
opinions and the other "unnecessary" bits of
humanness. I convinced myself I'd get it all back when
someone fell in love with me. Then, I thought, I'd be

whole again—but the butchering never stopped. I was so eager to be consumed, certain that in the bellies of those who desired me, I would find belonging. They were insatiable, though. Eventually, they grew full or tired of the way I tasted. I watched them leave, unmoved by my absence, as I stood there, breathless and bloody, a shell of myself. I wanted to scream. I wanted to run after them and shout,

"AFTER EVERYTHING I'VE DONE FOR YOU! *FOR YOU*! WHY DON'T YOU LOVE ME?!"

Over my sobs I heard the gritty voice of someone I had buried many years before. She had clawed her way back to the surface with a vengeance, and was not going to let me ignore her this time. Her cynical omnipotence coated the room in a heavy smoke. Grief had finally come for me.

"Did they ever even *know* you? Do *you* even know you?" She beckoned from behind me.

I had never looked Grief directly in the eye. In the ghost stories I was told as a child, she was a Medusa of sorts who would turn your heart to stone, freezing you from the inside out and trapping you in your greatest pain. As I laid there on the floor in my finest party dress, I was defeated by the realization that no amount of carefully calculated charm, perfectly balanced seductive wholesomeness, or even the desperate Hail Mary of a push-up bra could compel love. Grief's smoke filled my lungs and I decided I was ready to meet her icy grip. This pain would last forever, anyway, I thought. When I finally turned to face her, though, Grief was not how I imagined. Her touch was soft. She handed me a pen and gave me words to tell my stories with. In her honey-colored eyes I could see clearly. She wasn't surrounded by smoke, but fog, for it was morning. Awakened from the endless dark night I had entered so many years before, I realized the ghost stories were rumors told by those who had been too afraid of what the daylight would bring. I held her close and brushed the dirt from her shoulders. Grief took me by the hand and led me back to her old grave. We laughed like old friends as we buried the hatchets I once held as prized possessions. In her company, I forgot why I had kept them in the first place.We planted flowers as a love letter to all the boys I blamed before, and the bees turned their nectar into honey. When the day's work was done, Grief and I raised glasses of sweet tea to toast. Together, we turned the graveyard into a garden.

We marvel at great beauties like they're newfound treasures. We take them into the light and watch all of their edges glisten, fascinated by their curves unknown to us. We look, and look, and *look* until we decide the great beauty isn't so marvelous anymore. We didn't find what we were looking for. The truth of course is that, we weren't looking for anything in particular, were we? We just looked at the same great beauty everyday until it became commonplace to us, until it was old, until the edges no longer seemed shiny enough to hold our attention and we decided to take something else, something newer, something more promising into the light instead. But where do great beauties go when we're done looking at them? I'd like to think they go off in search of their own light.

Dallas Taylor

You may never stop loving them. You may wake up ten years from now and still hold them in your heart with tenderness. You may still find them beautiful and you might even miss their laugh, but do you want to know a beautiful, happy, marvelous secret? Love doesn't have to hurt. It doesn't have to remain as this ache within you, yearning and burning for them. It will not always be painful. One day, you're going to wake up and the spite will be gone. Don't mistake this for redemption, it's not. Don't call them thinking you were wrong to have hurt when they hurt you. The spite will be gone and it will give way to understanding—if not for them, then for yourself. The love that once ached within you will be replaced by a quiet fondness, a gentle remembrance between friends. The mark of the way you loved will linger, but it will not always be an open wound.

I Belong Deeply to Myself

I lovingly refer to the point after a breakup where you realize it's never going to be different as the second death. It's the moment when you understand the person was never going to treat you with more intention, magically wake up one day and know they were wrong, or decide you deserved better. Even worse, sometimes they'll realize it and *still* not show up at your doorstep with the apology or flowers you've convinced yourself you need. The thing is, the second death usually sets me free. It hurts almost worse than the initial heartbreak, because in many ways, it's the death of the hope you've clung to in an effort to avoid fully letting go. It requires us to fully acknowledge our pain, and say goodbye to an alternative reality we weren't quite ready to relinquish. That is real closure; to see someone had every chance to care about you, to show up for you and make their feelings known, and didn't. For me, the second death signifies a chapter closed, and frees me from the need to write alternate endings in my head.

I no longer find it exciting to be *wanted*. I possess the sort of warmth that draws people inward. The softness in my voice mirrors the one they found in their mother's when she used to call them in for dinner. The touch of my skin is as comforting as the floor of their childhood bedroom on a summer day. The way I listen reminds them of their kindergarten teacher; attentive, caring, and involved. I have a gift for making people feel safe enough to be themselves. It makes sense when people *want* me. But I am not your mother, an old room to revisit, or a teacher. My eyes are not two pools of honey waiting for flies to linger. So no, it's not impressive when someone *wants* me anymore—not when I know I deserve to be *cherished*.

I Belong Deeply to Myself

I'm getting better at acknowledging simultaneous truths. The truth is rarely a one-dimensional thing; People who love us deeply can hurt us immensely. We can be scared and courageous concurrently (really, we can't be one without the other). We can do our best, try our hardest, and *still fail*. I think all the best lessons I've learned have been found in the space between two truths. This space is where I've found compassion, both for myself and for others. It's where messy, romantic, wonderful, awful, incredible, mundane, excruciating, invigorating humanity lives. It's the gray area I've had to step into to sort through the muckier pieces of myself, and the walk-off homer I hit when the puzzle pieces click into place. The truth is a fickle lady with many faces, and a wicked enemy if you make one out of her. But when I finally let her be all of herself, all at once, I find her to be a powerful ally.

"If he wanted to he would." Why is it always about what *he* wants? Why is it not, "*I* do not want someone who cannot show up consistently," or, "*I* am not attracted to someone who cannot meet my basic needs," or, "*I* wanted a partner who matches my energy, so *I* found one." Women are taught, from a very young age, to view romance and love as things that *happen to us.* We are famed to be uncontrollably emotional creatures who have no will over the way we feel or express ourselves. The way we have been presented to ourselves requires us to unlearn these perspectives. Personally, I will never again measure my safety, satisfaction, or enjoyment based on my partner's level of interest in the relationship. Interest and accountability are the bare minimum. With those covered, what do *I* want?

I Belong Deeply to Myself

I was crushed at the thought of him not missing me. Of him not kicking himself over losing me. Then, I quietly came to the realization that someone who never took the time to know me, to understand me, to appreciate me, could never know the gravity of what he'd lost even if he tried. I'm sure he misses the way I did his laundry for him, or the way I made him feel like he wasn't a total and complete failure because he could use *my* beauty and *my* accomplishments as things that added value to *him* because I was *his*. I'm sure he misses the things I did for him, but he had no idea who I was outside of the version that existed to please him. So, how could he possibly miss *me*?

I'm sure you thought my world shattered when you left. I can understand why you would think that. People don't write sad poetry about things they're unaffected by. In a way, my world was shattered, but that's not the whole story. *A* world shattered when you left—the one I had built around you. I cut myself on broken glass and wept like a child at the remains of a crushed diorama, frightful for what I would have to present to the class in your absence. When the tears subsided, and the wounds healed, I remembered who the architect had been. Then, I started building again. This time, around myself.

I Belong Deeply to Myself

I can promise you this: if the sun sets on what you thought you wanted, if someone pulls the rug out from under you, or if you find yourself standing alone with an outstretched hand that was once held—the sun will rise again, and with it will come new colors and desires you'd never considered before. Your outstretched hand will reach for greater heights and you'll come to understand why it had to be free to grasp what you were meant for. Mourn your lost love. Feel your pain. Let it wash over you, then let it wash out.

One day I woke up and it didn't hurt anymore. Not because I had forgotten the pain, but because I had allowed myself to feel the grief. My past lovers were no longer cast as monsters in my memory, but rather finished chapters I need not revisit. The harshness I once held for them became coated with a rosy film, reflecting all the lessons I learned from them back to me. I was no longer afraid to run into them in public or hear their names from our friends. I realized they weren't evil-doers who had wronged me, they were at war with themselves, just like I had been, and we'd just been stuck in each other's crossfire.

Sometimes, people will find better. Not better *than* you, but better *for* them. The good news is,

you will, too.

The Conundrum of Early Adulthood

The conundrum of early adulthood is this: we finally have the freedom to be whoever we want, and yet, many of us are entirely unsure of who exactly that person is. We exist in duality—simultaneously carefree in the moment and dutifully committed to our futures. Our twenties are exhilarating, promising, and at times, incredibly lonely, because we're terrified to admit that the so-called best years of our lives don't always feel the best. When we refuse to admit it, we pretend—on social media and in bars, in relationships we don't feel good in and in jobs we are less-than-thrilled with. We pretend until we've isolated ourselves from the true gift of early adulthood; the other twenty-somethings who feel just as lost as we do. The pressure to somehow enjoy this time and also make the absolute most of it paralyzed me. I froze, incapable of making decisions because I was afraid I would choose incorrectly. I viewed my twenties as this island I had been stranded on, waiting for a rescue boat in the form of my dream job or perfect relationship to carry me to the stability promised in my thirties. I jumped into relationships and jobs I ultimately found unfulfilling, simply because I was afraid nothing better would come, then ended up right back where I had started. I decided if I was going to be stuck on this island, I needed a warm place to lay my head. When I looked around, I realized the land was fertile and the surrounding jungle lush. I just had to be brave enough to believe I deserved what it had to offer. So, I started building my own house. At first it was just a place to survive in, but soon, it became a place I enjoyed. I started to picture early adulthood less as an island I was stranded on, and more as a room I could decorate however I pleased. Decorating is an expression of who I am, and it doesn't happen overnight. It takes time to find the perfect lamp and dining room table to fit the space in the same way it takes time to find a job where I feel fulfilled and happy. I invite people in before my home is fully furnished, eating dinners with them out of takeout boxes on my floor, honestly telling them why there is no couch or boyfriend with a smile, "I just haven't found one I really like." We laugh in my kitchen and talk candidly about how hopeful and hopeless we are all at once. Eventually, there are framed photos on my walls, a job I love and people who love me back. There is a dining room table, a lover, a desk where I make things I am proud of, and a *life* that fits me—a home right here, on the island I once felt shipwrecked on.

I Belong Deeply to Myself

You're not waiting for your life to start. It's here, now, in the hometown that feels too small and in the new city that seems scary and foreign. It's in the breakups and the breakdowns, the wins and the losses. It's in the way you *really* fucked up this time and in the way that next time, (maybe) you won't! You're not in a waiting room. No one will call your name and invite you to the life you're so certain everyone else is living better than you. You've arrived. It's yours.

Now what will you do with it?

Dallas Taylor

I have found my mid-twenties feel like a department store dressing room. The lighting is harsh and the good options seem buried beneath piles of stuff that doesn't suit me. I'm trying things on for size-jobs, partners, cities, friendships—and many of them feel too small. You know the moment of panic in a fitting room where the item is just big enough to get on, but entirely uncomfortable and almost impossible to take off? You're by yourself, struggling to remove it without ripping the clothes or maiming yourself. That's how change in your mid-twenties feels. You sort through a plethora of less-than-desirable options to find something you think may work, only to find it is all wrong. It's almost just as uncomfortable to keep on as it is to take off. You peel it from your skin and maybe even have a few red marks from where it was especially too tight. You leave feeling discouraged, downtrodden, and too big (which you haven't discovered is a good thing, yet). The immediate response you want to have is to run for comfort, be it in an old lover, friend, habit, or place. In our mid-twenties, though, it's imperative we get comfortable being uncomfortable. It's the kindest thing we can do for ourselves, to have faith in our own ability to find comfort within, and the courage to keep trying things on.

I Belong Deeply to Myself

When we stop viewing life as a laundry list of things we *have to accomplish,* and rather as a collection of *experiences we get to have*, we give ourselves permission to sit back and enjoy the ride. I had been treating my life like a test I was desperate to pass, determined to control every outcome in my favor. Instead, I started treating my life like a concert. I don't tell the band what to play, I just show up, listen, enjoy myself, and try to meet a few people along the way who like the same kind of music I do.

I often wonder when the last day of my childhood was. Did it end with a bang at the last Ice-O-Plex birthday party? Did it dance its way out as "Ob-La-Di, Ob-La-Da" played for the final time while my friend and I rode in the backseat of his mom's Ford Excursion? No, I think it happened slowly, and then all at once, as my pretend game of house became a real one. I didn't realize it was gone until the first time I heard "Landslide" and understood it wasn't really about a mountain. I wish I could go back and tell my little self to hang on tightly to her imaginary world instead of burying it. It would have saved me a lot of digging.

Nostalgia is a beautiful liar. She whispers about our past in seductive tones that beckon us backwards, promising more desirable outcomes in her heavenly hindsight. When you find yourself being lured by her sweet familiarity, be grateful you have had a life full of people, places, and times worth missing, but remember *there is more.* You are meant to live a big, beautiful life. There are more people you will love, more places that will take your breath away, and more times you will surely miss. Nostalgia paints a pretty picture of the past, but she, at best, only tells half-truths. The whole truth is right here, right now in the present, which is where we'll find something much more beautiful than nostalgia: the incredible, fleeting gift of being alive.

My twenties have been a reclamation of the girlhood that was stolen from me. I dance around in non-sensible shoes. I stay up all night with my girlfriends chatting about world domination or gel extensions over pie. I do whatever the hell I like because *I can.* The people who tried to convince me to give up silly, wild, childish ways are the same ones who now watch me in awe and wonder where my power comes from. I laugh because, of course, it comes from her—the fourteen year old girl they tried so desperately to hide from herself.

When I was 5, I counted how many years were between me and 10 so I could just reach double digits. Then, when I was 13, I longed to be 16 so I could drive. At 16, I wanted to be 18 so I could make my own decisions. At 18, I couldn't *wait* to be 21 so I could *finally* go out to a bar. At 21, I would tell myself, "just two more years until we're done with college." Something happened when I turned 25, though. Here I was, with double digits, a driver's license, making my own decisions with my college degree in any bar of my choosing. Suddenly I realized I hadn't learned how to *enjoy* my life, I'd only learned how to get through it. That was the beginning of a very important self-reckoning for me. I stopped waiting for the next benchmark to bring my life meaning. Instead, I decided what gave my life meaning was that it was *mine*, and I was determined to enjoy every moment of it to the best of my ability.

Half your friends start marrying their long term partners, and the other half get taken across the country for a promotion. Everyone watches each other make life altering decisions, fearfully hoping they themselves have made the right one. I watched my friends move away, get married, and have babies, while I wondered when my ticket to the next event would come—the partner to sweep me off my feet or the job to whisk me away—unaware I was allowed to enjoy a moment of stillness in the tumultuous chaos that comes with figuring out who it is you want to be once you realize you are entirely your own.

I Belong Deeply to Myself

Our parents sold our childhood homes, and I heard they're putting up a strip mall where the old drive-in used to be. Did you hear the alumni are already planning a reunion? I grab coffee at the shop beneath my apartment, thousands of miles from where you'll grab yours. Remember when we used to do this in the same place at the same time? In my city, there are lights that never go out, subways, greasy pizzas, brick apartments and all-night diners. In yours, there are pine trees and mountains, tropical storms and lush green land, golden coasts and Hollywood stars, babies and spouses, hometown haunts and the best donuts I miss dearly.

When you visit me, we'll eat greasy pizza in my brick apartment the way we held hands at graduation: *together*.

When I visit you, we'll drive around and eat our favorite donuts, hike through the pines, jump in the ocean, drive down Sunset, or kiss your babies the same way we ran back to each other's houses over Christmas break: *finally*.

For now, I'll drink my coffee with honey the same way you used to make it for me in our first apartment. You'll turn on *Gilmore Girls* and remember how I always sang the theme.

In any city, we'll always find pieces of each other.

I decided to allow myself the pleasure of being just a little bit reckless. I gave myself permission to fall in love even if it meant being heartbroken later, to quit jobs even if it meant not having a plan for a while. I was heartbroken for a bit. I maybe still sort of am, but I'm figuring it out as I go along. I ditched the plan and created a new one that suited me better. I drove across the country, across the plains of Texas and through the Smoky Mountains of Tennessee. I danced through the French Quarter and remembered every single fuck up I'd allowed myself in the last two years—every risk, every failure, every tear-stained night—was now an experience in my tool box I could use to create a really beautiful life that felt like it belonged to *me* and no one else. I plan on fucking up a lot more, because as I now know, fuck ups are capital. They're the currency with which we obtain the incredibly valuable resource of life experience. They become the cautionary tales we tell our grandchildren and the once-embarrassing moments we laugh at with friends. Mistakes, wrong turns, and the fuck ups make our stories worth reading.

I Belong Deeply to Myself

Drink this in. Bathe in the seemingly insurmountable uncertainty surrounding you and relish this feeling of being lost. One day soon, you're going to wake up and the same places that once felt boundless will feel familiar and ordinary. Embrace the subtle buzzing inside of you urging you to push harder and further into the rest of who you are. Notice the itch crawling beneath your skin as your soul extends into every inch of your incredible, improbable, beautiful existence. Let yourself be scared, devastated, hopeful, honest, silly, wild, and wistful. Enjoy the revolving doors, the free falling, the spinning arms wide open. Take a jump even if it means hitting the ground hard. The wind knocked out of you will become that which floats beneath your wings.

Know you deserve to fail *and* fly—and you can rarely do one without the other.

We move to new cities and try our hands at new love, with heartbreak in the breast pockets of ill-fitting suit jackets paid for on limited credit cards. We step into shoes much too big only to jump into a seemingly limitless pond, where before we remember how to swim, we float. We learn some of the faces we thought were fixtures were actually fleeting, *beautiful and temporary*. And we realize it all is; beautiful but temporary—these moments of uncertainty, confusion, hope, fear, potential, risk, love, failure, laughter and success—and we owe it to ourselves to take it all in before it's gone.

Stop spending so much time thinking about *who* loves you and start spending it on *what* you love to do. The *who* will show up among the *what*.

When we were small, we struggled through our first steps. Now, we walk, run, and dance without giving those first shaky steps a second thought. Healing is like that. You will fall down. You will sometimes regress back to a crawl when your legs feel shaky and crawling feels safer. You'll want to retreat back into the arms of ex-lovers who may not appreciate you but whose arms feel familiar. You'll doubt yourself until one day, you don't. You'll just be healed, as if you always were. Then, you'll find new wounds to tackle just like you found bike riding and ballet. Healing isn't linear, it's an ever-evolving skill we cultivate in different forms.

I Belong Deeply to Myself

My limbs used to ache as they grew. I'd feel the slow and brutal lengthening of bones and the tightness of my skin expanding like canvas stretched over a new framework. I cried as I outgrew my pink sparkly shoes and butterfly jeans, cursing my mother as she replaced them with others that fit me better and passed my prized possessions off in a hand-me-down bag. Eventually, my body reached its final width and height and the soreness subsided. Then, my soul started to grow, too. I cried again, outgrowing people and places, this time letting them go with love, quietly missing them but knowing we would both find someone else to fit us better. At 23, I laid in bed writhing the same way I had at 10, 11, and 12, desperate for comfort, and my bones whispered, "Remember, it's only temporary, and you'll be bigger for it." I felt the pains again at 24, 25, and 26. Now, I greet them with a grateful sigh. What a gift it is to keep growing.

You sit on the floor of an apartment that doesn't really feel like home, with your head in your hands as you think, "This is *supposed* to be the *best* time of my life." What if this is as good as it gets? What if you're wasting this time? What if? What if? *What if?*

What if, possibly, this is the time where you learn how to breathe deeply in the face of fear?

What if instead of trying to figure out what you want to do with your entire life at the very beginning of it, you figure out what brings you joy?

What if you started making choices based on what felt authentic to *you*, rather than what you feel you're *supposed* to choose?

What if you decided your twenties don't need to be the *best* time of your life, they just need to be *yours?*

You may start to feel at home (*and I don't just mean in the apartment*).

Real Love Knows Boundaries

I thought that "real love" was a love without boundaries, but that was before I learned boundaries are not walls meant to keep us from knowing each other, but rather bridges meant to bring us closer together with people who mean us no harm. Boundaries require respect, met expectations, and honesty. *Real* love knows boundaries.

My ego finds fear romantic. It doesn't listen when people become prophets as they whisper, "I don't deserve you." It decides they need some of our light to see, breaking off a piece of our opal-colored aura as a gesture of good faith, as if to say, "You won't lose me." Of course, the prophets are right. They take my light and drink my wine until I'm left with darkness and empty bottles, a shell that echoes their smug, "I told you so," as they leave.

Go where you are deserved.

Stop spending time with people who look into your eyes and don't grasp the multitudes of miracles it took for you to exist *exactly as you are.* Take lovers who speak to their God in tongues, praying to spend every mundane afternoon beside you. Find friends who would cross oceans to see you happy, even if only for a moment. Find people who watch you stumble and admire the grace with which you rise again. The people who treat us as if we are extraordinary at our kitchen tables far before we arrive at mountain tops or podiums are the ones who are meant to be beside us—because in truth, we are.

I Belong Deeply to Myself

I think a lot of us have forgotten we are supposed to *like our friends*. Not just their photos, videos, and stories. We are supposed to light up when we see them, whether it's by chance in a grocery store or by design online. There are 7,942,645,086 people in the world *right now*. That means there are roughly 7,942,645,085 chances for each of us to find people who really love, understand, and celebrate us. So if I unfollow you, or if we part ways, it's not because I hate you. It's because I believe you deserve a chance to find people who will stop and ask you how you've been when they run into you in the frozen aisle. You deserve people who see the life you've made for yourself online and smile. You deserve to be *celebrated,* and so do I.

We were never supposed to watch the lives of our former friends and lovers play out in tiny squares online. We weren't supposed to be allowed a portal into their happiest moments because at one point, we imagined ourselves in those moments *beside* them. When you date and break up, or have a falling out with a friend, the only window you're supposed to have into their lives is the memory of the life you shared together. It isn't healthy to keep tabs on the ghosts that haunt our daydreams or the menaces that bring us melancholy. You will be disappointed *every single time*, because as much as you want to open their page to find them begging for you back, or kicking themselves over your being gone, you won't. You'll find a summary of their happiest, shiniest moments, carefully curated to communicate *exactly* what they want it to. Sure, there's always the chance the person will wander back into your life, but do you really need to stick around and watch what they do from afar until then?

The kinship I have found between myself and other women is unlike any other love I've ever known, and I feel like it isn't celebrated with enough splendor. The proverbial drunk girls of bar bathrooms with extra tampons or kind words to spare made the gray area of my early twenties less lonely. The women I am fortunate enough to call friends have watched me fuck up and then helped me laugh about it later. They have forgiven me for the mistakes I have made while becoming. You see, it has always been women who have held my hair and fixed it into a braid so even my lowest moments could feel beautiful in some way. They danced with me down broken roads and made me who I am. So when I say, "I am *just like other girls*," I am proud. I am a mosaic of the women who have lent me some of their light. Light I would not have found my way without.

Everything I've learned about love—real, true, tender, unconditional love—I've learned from women. They have been the ones to take me, and celebrate me, as I have been, am, and will be. I saw it in their eyes when they knew what was wrong before I could say it. I tasted it in the meals they cooked for me with recipes passed down from their mothers, and their mother's mothers before them. I heard it in the way they cheered for me, not because they had any stake in my success, but because my winning brought them joy. I smelled it in their floral perfume as they told me, "Thank you! I got it on sale at..." Most of all, I felt it when they cried with me. When they laughed with me. When those who had come before me cradled my broken body so I might know how to hold the ones who were sure to follow.

I have been lied to and cheated in the pursuit of love. I have been rejected and discarded trying to convince others I was worthy of keeping. Even still, I am a devout believer in the power of love. I have seen what love can do because it was love who picked me up and put my broken pieces back together. It was love who let me cry on her shoulder and hold her hand when I was weak. Love stood by me and propped me up when I had mistaken the impostors of lust, longing, deceit and betrayal for her. Love was in the eyes of my friends who watched me cry and felt my pain in the pit of their stomachs. It was in the hands of their babies who grabbed my finger and reminded me that love is innocent, pure, and simple. Love is not my enemy, she is the means by which I survived, and I will always believe in her.

I used to curse my sensitivity. I was afraid it would overwhelm people. I thought of it as my Achilles' heel, a wound I must keep hidden so as not to appear weak to my opponents. Though, as I've healed, I've realized my sensitivity is what makes me intuitive, empathetic, warm, and connective. It is the superpower that helps me find *my* people—the ones who meet me with eyes, arms, and hearts wide open.

This love I've found, it's evergreen. It's endless and it's patient. It sees me through my dark times and it holds my hand when things get scary. It's an early Sunday morning with pancakes and coffee just because, and it *never* lies because we have no secrets. It's honest when it needs to be, but it's never harsh or judgmental. This love is slow and steady and I know that no matter what, at the end of the day, we'll be okay. This love I've found is timeless and peaceful, a homecoming after a long time away where your room looks the same but you suddenly have a newfound fondness for the way it makes you feel safe. This love is everything I have been looking for and more.

How funny to think it was right there within me all this time.

I used to feel guilty for expecting reciprocity in my relationships, because I thought sharing my love should feel selfless, like gift giving. I was convinced giving my time, love, care, and affection away in the hopes of receiving some back would somehow make the acts less genuine. Now, I view relationships less as gift giving and more as a potluck. Sometimes you bring an entree and your friend brings the wine. Other times you'll bring dessert and they'll handle the main course. You take turns bringing more to the table.

Everybody eats.

I hope when you light the candles on the table, you do it because it brings you joy. I hope the people you break bread with are the ones who want to see you win, and who celebrate you for the person you are. I hope you remember that though the holidays may have once meant slammed doors and dagger-eyed fights at the table, you can create new traditions. You can make them *better.* You can make them *yours.*

Love is your birthright. You need not earn it.

For so long I tried to accomplish rest. I would make lists of things I needed to do to relax, with elaborate skin care routines and guided meditations. When I finally gave myself permission to do absolutely nothing, I learned how to stop viewing a window of open time as a failure or lapse in productivity. Setting boundaries with other people, but more importantly with myself transformed me. I stopped talking to myself like I wasn't worthy of rest and allowed myself to cultivate the skill of slowing to a gentle stop, rather than falling from a full sprint.

We have to give people the opportunity to show up for us the way we want them to. Even the people who love us dearly cannot read our minds. We have to be willing to be vulnerable, set boundaries, and communicate our needs, then let people respond in whatever way is most authentic to their truth. People won't always be able to meet us where we are. Not everyone is going to understand you—but you still deserve to be understood. Give people a chance to honor your wants, needs, and boundaries, then release them with love if they're not able to deliver.

The kindest thing we can do for ourselves and others is be honest about the way we feel, and then allow them to do the same.

I Belong Deeply to Myself

I've never been able to relate when people use the phrase, "*more than words*," to describe the way they love someone. Though I understand the sentiment, I've never met something I couldn't describe in painstaking detail. Maybe I haven't really loved—or maybe, I'm meant to tell people exactly how the feeling I have for them is akin to looking into the face of a tidal wave and deciding to swim. How in the sound of their voice I find the kind of warmth I thought only existed on my mother's couch. Maybe, I'm meant to be the one to narrate the tale of when their hand met the small of my back, and the entire universe paused just long enough for my mind to turn us into two live wires, tangled up like electric eels wrapped in metaphor. Maybe there is *nothing* I love more than words—which is why my giving them away is a profound act of love in and of itself.

You know what tastes better than skinny feels? A slice of my best friend's wedding cake. The soup I made before sitting down to watch *Practical Magic* when it was cold outside. Vegetables because I like them, not because they're one of "10 foods to eat for a tiny waist." The Good Humor strawberry shortcake bar that tastes like playing catch in the street with my dad as the ice cream truck rolled by "unexpectedly." Letting the sun touch every inch of my body like a tender hand rather than an interrogative lamp. Not paying attention to the way the curve of my stomach looks in a pair of jeans. Living and loving with a fullness I could've never found when I was determined to be *less*.

Gratitude doesn't have to indicate stagnancy, and ambition is not synonymous with dissatisfaction. The two experiences are not mutually exclusive. The space where we find gratitude and ambition side by side is a special, happy place called *fulfillment.*

There is one thing I know to be absolutely certain; I deserve a love I don't have to make excuses for. I deserve a love story that doesn't need to be trimmed to disguise the gaps where I was mistreated. I deserve to be loved by someone who keeps their word, who shows up when they say they're going to, and wants me mind, body, and soul. I know I deserve it because I *am* that love.

I deserve to be loved by someone like me.

I was 10 when I became aware of my body. Suddenly, with the eyes of men lingering just a little too long, and my mother's gentle "that's enough," after my first helping of ice cream, I learned my body no longer belonged to me. It was to be meticulously maintained and pristinely preserved, like an artifact in a museum dedicated to my youthful hairlessness and girlish shape. It was to be desired but *never* obtained, a chaste temple that inspired pleasure, but need not partake. My entire young adult life would be dedicated to shaping, contouring, plucking, tanning, whitening, lifting, and altering my body for the sake of being *seen*. The body positivity movement only made me more aware of the days when I *didn't* feel good about myself. At 25, I realized what I really wanted wasn't to wake up and love my body, it was to wake up and feel the way I did when I was 9;

blissfully unaware of the shell my soul walked around in.

I Belong Deeply to Myself

The girl in the mirror stares back at me wondering why I am so wretched to her. "Your limbs aren't long enough," I scoff, "Your face is too narrow and your skin is too speckled. Your stomach protrudes too far and your legs are too wide." I watch her inch away from me, further and further until there is no one there at all. I'm an empty shell of skin and bone, my only friends the ribs now protruding from my side. If this is beauty, why does it feel so ugly? If this is success, why do I feel as though I've failed? Because I have. I have failed myself. My body—*my* body—is not a token to present to the world, hoping they will find it desirable *enough* to spend it like spare change. It is not a commodity to be used up or a temple to worship in. It is a garden I must nurture for longevity, vibrance, and sanctuary. It is the only place in the world where I am completely alone, the only place that will ever belong to me and me only.

I deserve to love that place.

I dreamt of the daughter I would have and the way I would brush her hair and sing to her. I smiled thinking of the birthday parties I would throw for her, and the way I would teach her what love was supposed to look like so she wouldn't go looking for it in the wrong places. I looked at her imaginary little life as a second chance at the one I felt had escaped me. I'll admit I was envious of her. Like my mother and her mother before her, I was shouting at the top of my lungs, "DO YOU NOT KNOW HOW LUCKY YOU ARE?" I was jealous of a life that hadn't happened yet. I started gently brushing my own hair and throwing myself birthday parties with triple tier cakes and streamers. I sang to myself as I decorated my home and taught myself about the kind of love that wouldn't hurt us. I found the little girl who had really needed someone like me right where I had left her all those years ago. I walked her home, tucked her in, and let her dream of something else entirely.

I am cringe. I am crazy. I laugh too loudly and trip over my feet. On my best days I'm a mess of dark hair, big love, and a sharp wit. On my worst I'm unfair, harsh, and too quick to speak or judge. But on both days, I am trying. I am laughing at myself. I am holding myself accountable (even if it's in retrospect). I am admitting when I'm hurt, scared, happy, or hopeful. I am learning how to love things that are good for me, leave things that aren't, and how to tell the difference between the two. I am deciding that actually, I am enough and there is time. I am trying, and I am failing. On both days, I am getting better.

Healing, to me, is somewhat like walking into a dusty, old attic crowded with things you'd rather leave out of sight. The work of healing is sorting through garbage and heirlooms alike to figure out what's worth examining more closely, what you need to let go of, and even finding a few treasures you didn't know you had. Things start spilling out onto the floor and soon there's disorder all around you, because it gets worse before it gets better. Spiders crawl out from the cracks and scare you. You feel frustrated, overwhelmed, and agitated. The more you start to make sense of the mess, though, the lighter you feel. You start to find a place for the feelings that still have lessons to teach you, and you give away the ones that don't. You smile at the memory of old loves and cry at tattered photos of your grandmother. You open the window to let the light in and the spiders out. Soon, you find you have much more space than you thought you did, bringing new memories in with the light. You don't stop healing just as you don't stop throwing junk in the attic. You just revisit what you've learned and apply it in different ways, reminding yourself you're capable, even when things may seem overwhelming.

People start to notice when you've found peace within yourself. They can't quite put their finger on it, but there's something enigmatic about you. You are quiet, but still demand to be heard. You're not fighting, but you're assertive. That's because there is a magnetism associated with the gentle knowing of who you are by no one else's standards but your own. When you decide you belong deeply to yourself, you gain an unshakable foundation beneath your feet, rooted wherever you go, with new growth and branches constantly emerging up above you without a second thought. Growth is no longer something you *try* to do, it's just something that happens as if it always has, because in reality, *it always was*.

Let people think you're crazy. Let people think they've gotten the best of you. Let them believe whatever they need to and focus on *your* truth. Who are you, to you? Are you truly unhappy with yourself, or are you just unhappy with the reflection you see mirrored in the eyes of people you have decided are a better authority on you than yourself? Chances are, when it all falls away, you won't feel crazy. You won't feel too loud or too big or too much at all, because you'll end up *exactly* where you belong.

I Belong Deeply to Myself

When we encounter joy, love, and happiness, we don't question them, we just enjoy the way they wash over us. When we meet grief, anger, or sadness, though, we turn them into professors, meant to enlighten us in some way. But sometimes, the point of loss is to lose. Sometimes, the point of pain is to hurt. Your emotions don't have to serve a higher purpose to be important. You deserve to feel, not for what you'll learn from it, but because you are *human*.

Feeling is why we are here.

The world needs to see the bumps in our noses and the chips in our teeth. As a little girl, I would've been happy to see a woman on the cover of a magazine who wasn't embracing her flaws so much as she was believing they weren't flaws in the first place. Who decided my teeth needed to be perfectly straight and white? When did the jury rule my hair must be smooth and shiny? Who is the authority on how many inches across my hips should span or how high my cheekbones should sit? Beauty lies not in the eyes of the beholder, but in the honesty of humanity. In the mess on my bedroom floor and the way I sometimes trip over my feet after too much tequila. It lives in the scar on my lip from when my sixth grade crush and I collided during a feverish game of kickball and the fact that I have stories to tell is what makes me *beautiful*.

I Belong Deeply to Myself

The greatest gift I ever gave myself was *permission;*

To explore

To pursue joy

To quit jobs I hated

To make art

To be content

To be angry

To admit when I am wrong

To fail

To fall in love

To be alone

And to remember that growth is not always a flower,

Sometimes, it's a seed.

For the first time in my life, I believe wholeheartedly in my own goodness. I am not spun together with gold and I am not without flaw. I have been judgmental, mean, and callous at times. I've said the wrong thing and embarrassed myself. I've lied, cheated, and made mistakes that hurt people. Even still, I am worthy of love. Maybe even more so now than ever, because I know the value of the girl who stands before the world. Her goodness is not rooted in the absence of bad; it comes from the fact that, though she is capable of bad things, she continues to *choose* goodness wherever she can. I believe in my own goodness because I have watched it go to bat with my bad and win, time and time again.

You are not meant to be half-loved. You are a symphony of blood, sweat, and tears, a thousand faces from a thousand years inherited in one smile. You are a gift of karma and sacrifice bound in earthly flesh and bone, a soul tethered to this world by a few ligaments and tendons. Your mercurial existence in itself is a birthmark of divine timing and glorious happenstance, the universe sighing with every breath you draw inward and release. You are not meant to be half-loved.

You are already whole.

When my words evade me, when they hide in the cracks of my mind like crabs between the rocks, I let them. I used to go after them, squeezing myself into their hiding places that were always much too small and dark, only ever emerging with useless handfuls of mismatched phrases. I have learned that, like love, my words prefer to show up with an element of surprise, and that they rarely come out of their hiding place without the bait of a life well-lived. When they make themselves scarce, I make myself more alive. I swim in the sea and fill my lungs with mountain air. I eat food that tastes like a warm hug, and notice it's gone cold while I was laughing with my friend about nothing in particular. I read books about faeries and shapeshifters and get lost on trains to unfamiliar cities. I dance and sing and kiss and cry and draw and spin and *live*. When I finally look up, I realize my words are there, watching me, waiting to be woven together. After all, it is my life that gives them meaning—not the other way around.

I Belong Deeply to Myself

I smile as the books beside my bed pile up next to my glass of water (decidedly) half-full. My laundry remains unfolded for a few days, my empty wine glass has lipstick around the rim, and I believe there's something incredibly beautiful in feeling safe enough to be messy. I have made a life where mascara runs freely down faces and settles beneath tired eyes when it needs to. Things spill onto the floor when we're dancing and we pay it no mind until the party is over. No one is expected to be perfect and no one wants to be. No one yells at the sight of spilt milk or mistakes. We are *all* of ourselves in this house. Especially the messy parts.

I wake up in a clean apartment with hardwood floors creaking lovingly under my feet en route to a tea kettle. A cat brushes up against my leg to say good morning and the dog looks up at me with her big brown eyes, ready to roll around in the grass outside. My sister makes us our usual breakfast. Where once a cacophony of slammed doors, broken glass and raised voices played on repeat, there is now music, laughter with friends, and kept promises. I have a date at 7:30 with someone who makes me laugh.

She adores me.

She is beautiful.

She is *me*.

I Belong Deeply to Myself

On nights when you ache to belong, when you're tired, when you've been wrong, I hope these words help you remember:

It is to yourself you must surrender.

For every dark and wretched night, there is a morning that brings new light. When it all falls down, begin again, if you get lost, lean on your friends. Speak your mind, dare to feel, don't get caught up in the highlight reel. Know you're worthy of a love that's good, know you deserve to be understood. You will hurt, and you will fail, that's how you learn to fly and heal. You will grow in stillness too, flowers begin at the root. Rest is an oath to ourselves we must keep, and the art of slowness has much to teach. Real love is sometimes yes, and sometimes no, other times it is letting go. Life has no finish line, there is only enjoyment or wasted time. Drink it in, soak up your youth, accept your faults and learn your truth. Say you're sorry, write the love letter, we'll always do worse before we know better.

Know that we belong indeed,

You belong to you, and I belong to me.

TAYLOR OF CONTENTS

To Taylor Swift, whose music has always been, to me,
the sound of the world making sense, *thank you*.

1. Proximity to the Undoing of Love
-Right Where You Left Me
-Sad, Beautiful, Tragic (Taylor's Version)
-Happiness
-Champagne Problems
-Marjorie
-Seven
-Evermore
-Hoax
-Peace
-Bigger Than The Whole Sky

2. Fine! I Care! A Lot!
-Mirrorball
-Mastermind
-This Is Me Trying
-Cowboy Like Me

3. The Second Heartbreak
-Dear John (Taylor's Version)
-I Forgot That You Existed
-We Are Never Ever Getting Back Together (Taylor's Version)
-'Tis The Damn Season
-Tolerate It
-Exile
-I Almost Do
-The Way I Loved You (Taylor's Version)
-Mean (Taylor's Version)
-My Tears Ricochet

4. The Third Heartbreak
-Begin Again (Taylor's Version)
-The 1
-Renegade
-All Too Well (10 Minute Version) (Taylor's Version)
-I Bet You Think About Me (Taylor's Version) (From The Vault)
-Last Kiss (Taylor's Version)
-Should've Said No (Taylor's Version)
-Death By A Thousand Cuts

-Come Back, Be Here (Taylor's Version)
-You're Not Sorry (Taylor's Version)
-Holy Ground (Taylor's Version)
-Better Man (Taylor's Version) (From The Vault)
-August
-The Moment I Knew (Taylor's Version)
-Betty
-Red (Taylor's Version)
-Cardigan
-It's Time To Go
-Mr. Perfectly Fine (Taylor's Version) (From The Vault)
-Question…?
-Out Of The Woods (Taylor's Version)
-State Of Grace (Acoustic Version) (Taylor's Version)
-False God
-Getaway Car

5. To All The Boys I Blamed Before
-The Archer
-Clean (Taylor's Version)
-Long Story Short
-Coney Island
-Anti-Hero
-Bejeweled

6. The Conundrum of Early Adulthood
-A Place In This World (Taylor's Version)
-Welcome to New York (Taylor's Version)
-Wonderland (Taylor's Version)
-New Romantics (Taylor's Version)
-Wildest Dreams (Taylor's Version)
-You're On Your Own, Kid

7. Real Love Knows Boundaries
-Long Live (Taylor's Version)
-When Emma Falls In Love (Taylor's Version)
-Labyrinth
-I'm Only Me When I'm With You (Taylor's Version)

8. I Belong Deeply to Myself
-Dear Reader
-This Love (Taylor's Version)
-Daylight
-Karma

ABOUT THE AUTHOR

Dallas Taylor is a California born, Brooklyn-based writer who hopes her words help you feel less alone in times of turmoil, heartbreak, transition, and triumph. With a degree in Communications and an emphasis in Critical Cultural Media Studies, Dallas is passionate about the way words have the power to shape our world. Her belief is that the stories we tell ourselves matter greatly, for they become the narratives we live in. She is proud to live in these words, and she hopes you feel at home in them, too.

@dallastaylorrr on IG
@funauntiedal on TikTok

ACKNOWLEDGMENTS

To my therapist, without whom I would not be alive. To my sweet friends, who made me brave enough to share, believed in me, supported me, learned with me, answered my phone calls and whose conversations inspired the reflections you read in these pages. To my parents, who have healed with, supported, and loved me. To my chosen family, who had no obligation, but still showed up. To my hometown neighbors in Oceanside, the community that raised me and continues to cheer me on. To the boys who taught me how to love and lose. To my beloved Brooklyn neighbors who welcomed a heartbroken girl to the neighborhood with a, "Hey Hollywood!" To Ali at my favorite bodega, Natural Market on Quincy & Bedford, who gave me free candy when he could tell I was especially down. To my single girlfriends who laugh with me, cry with me, and still believe in love with me. To Nikki Gomez, who designed the cover and made my coffee with honey. To my sister, Kate McCall, who is my creative partner and best friend. To Kate, Morgan, and Sydney for moving with me across the country into a New York winter. To the people on TikTok, especially my fellow heartbroken girls in the summer of 2022, who read my words and let me know I wasn't alone.

Thank you, endlessly.